WILL ROGERS
American Humorist

Will Rogers

"Shucks, I was just an old cowhand that had a little luck. Why all this here fuss about me?"

WILL ROGERS
American Humorist

By Peter Anderson

CHILDRENS PRESS®

CHICAGO

PHOTO CREDITS

Courtesy of Will Rogers Memorial, Claremore, Oklahoma — cover, 6, 7, 8, 9, 10, 11 (right), 12, 17, 24, 27, 30 (left)
The Bettmann Archive — 1, 3, 11 (left), 15, 16, 20, 25 (right), 26, 28 (left), 31, 32
AP/Wide World Photos — 2, 13, 19, 25 (left), 28 (right), 29, 30 (top), 30 (right)
Culver — 5, 22, 23

EDITORIAL STAFF

Project Editor: E. Russell Primm III
Design and Electronic Composition: Biner Design
Photo Research: Carol Parden

Library of Congress Cataloging-in-Publication Data

Anderson, Peter, 1956–
    Will Rogers : American humorist / by Peter Anderson.
    p. cm. — (Picture-story biographies)
    Summary: Follows the life of the cowboy of Cherokee Indian descent who became a popular performer on stage and screen and a noted humorist.
    ISBN 0-516-04183-5
    1. Rogers, Will, 1879–1935—Juvenile literature. 2. Entertainers—United States—Biography—Juvenile literature. 3. Humorists, American—Biography—Juvenile literature. [1. Rogers, Will, 1879–1935. 2. Entertainers. 3. Humorists. 4. Cherokee Indians—Biography. 5. Indians of North America—Biography.] I. Title. II. Series.

PN2287.R74A84 1992	91-35057
792.7′028′092—dc20	CIP
[B]	AC

ON APRIL 27, 1905, something unexpected happened at a wild west show in New York City's Madison Square Garden. In the middle of the performance, an eight-hundred-pound steer smashed through a fence and rushed into the arena. Then it crashed through a guardrail and jumped into the stands. People ran up the aisles shouting and screaming.

Had it not been for a young cowboy named Will Rogers, somebody might have been seriously hurt, even killed. Will ran up the aisles chasing the wild steer. He twirled his lasso above his

Will Rogers in the Ziegfield Follies

head and threw a loop of rope around the animal's horns. The steer bucked and tugged but Will yanked on the rope and held on tight.

The next day, pictures of Will Rogers covered the front pages of all the newspapers in the city. "Indian Cowboy's Quickness Prevents Harm," read a headline in the *New York Herald*.

Will Rogers, the "Indian Cowboy," was proud of his heritage. His parents were both part Cherokee. Will was born in Indian Territory, which is now

A baby picture of Will Rogers

This is the house where Will Rogers was born. His parents' room where he was born is the first window on the right above the children.

the state of Oklahoma, on November 4, 1879. Not long after he learned to walk, Will was riding a pony. One day, Uncle Dan Walker, a ranch hand who worked for Will's father, showed Will how to throw a rope. From then on, Will was roping everything in sight — even his mother. One day she told him to quit roping in the house. He threw his lasso over her head and drew it tight around

This is the only existing picture of Mary America Rogers, Will's mother.

her arms. He would only let her go if she promised not to spank him.

Mary America Rogers was especially fond of her only son. He often made her smile. And Will loved her more than anyone in the world. So it came as a great shock when she died after a short sickness not long after Will's tenth birthday.

Clement Vann Rogers did his best to help his four children through this hard time. Will seemed to suffer the most. Long after the rest of the family had recovered, Will was still grieving. One day, Clem came up with a plan to help his son. He surprised Will with a wonderful gift — a beautiful buckskin pony named Comanche. Then he encouraged Will to ride hard and help with the ranch work. The harder Will worked, the better he felt, and the better he became at riding and roping.

Clem Vann Rogers, Will's father

9

Now that he was a ranch hand, Will figured he might not have to bother with school. But Clem Rogers wanted his son to get a good education. He sent Will to several different schools. Will spent more time with his ropes and horses, however, than he did with his books. At the age of eighteen, after

Will (center) and two of his buddies at Scarritt, one of the schools he attended

(left) After Scarritt, Will was sent to Kemper Military School in Boonville, Missouri. (above) Although Will loved roping most of all, he also enjoyed playing football on the Kemper team.

a year and a half at Kemper Military School, Will decided that he had been in school long enough. He wandered down to Higgins, Texas, where he got a job as a horse wrangler.

When Will returned to Oklahoma later that spring, Clem asked him if he would run the ranch. For a while, Will was glad to help out. But he was too restless to settle down.

One day he rode to the train depot in a nearby town and met Betty Blake, a pretty young girl who was visiting from Arkansas. For several months, they saw each other at parties and dances. When Betty left later that year, Will missed her terribly. He wrote her love letters — signing them "your true friend and Injun Cowboy, W. P. Rogers." But Betty never wrote back.

Betty Blake, the future Mrs. Will Rogers, at age 18

Will Rogers (far left) and a group of friends in 1900. Betty Blake is seated on the front seat with her hand to her chin.

Will saw her once again at a fair in Arkansas, but he felt shy and had little to say.

Then Will began to wander again. He had heard about Argentina's endless grasslands. There a cowboy could ride all day and night without seeing a fence. That kind of open range was getting harder to find in Oklahoma, so Will left for Argentina with his friend Dick Parris. Their sea

voyage was a roundabout one, first to
England and then on to Argentina. Will
and Dick rode out into the ranch
country they had heard so much about.
The land was beautiful but jobs were
scarce. Not knowing how to speak
Spanish made it even harder to find
work. Dick gave up and went back to
Oklahoma. Will decided to stay, but he
soon ran out of money.

He went to the city of Buenos Aires,
hoping that he would have better luck.
One day he noticed some men who
were trying to catch some mules in a
corral. Will couldn't resist the
temptation to show off a little. Besides,
he was broke and hungry. He borrowed
a rope and lassoed the mules, one after
another. The boss hired him on the spot.
After all the mules were taken care of,
Will was offered another job. A ship full
of livestock was leaving for South

Will often found creative and unusual ways to demonstrate his roping skills. Here he stands on the back of a steer while he twirls his lariat.

Africa. Someone was needed to take care of the horses and cattle.

Will didn't especially want to go to South Africa. But he needed the money, so he accepted the job. Soon, he wished he hadn't. He was seasick the whole time. It seemed as though the ocean would never end.

South Africa was a welcome sight. Will took a ranch job with the man who had shipped over the livestock. One day, while driving a herd of mules to the South African city of Ladysmith, he met an American named Texas Jack. Texas Jack's Wild West Show had been performing throughout Africa. After Will demonstrated a few of his favorite roping tricks, Texas Jack hired him to ride in the show.

Roping was one of Will's greatest pleasures. This is one of the many pictures of him with a rope in his hand.

Will Rogers shown in his traveling suit at the time he was appearing both on Broadway and in theaters around the United States.

For several months, Will traveled with Texas Jack's show. Billed as "The Cherokee Kid," he became one of the show's featured performers. Audiences loved his riding and roping tricks. In his spare time, Will even roped a few wild zebras.

Then he heard about an American circus that was touring through Australia and New Zealand. Will was anxious to return to the United States and figured he might as well see

another country on his way. So he said
goodbye to Texas Jack.

After another long boat ride, he met
up with the circus in New Zealand.
They hired him to ride and rope. Soon
he had enough money to pay for a
ticket back to San Francisco.

By the time Will returned to
Oklahoma in the spring of 1904, Will's
father hoped his son would settle down
and run the ranch. But Will had other
ideas. He wanted to be a performer.

Sensing his father's anger and
disappointment, Will agreed to run the
ranch until the cattle were ready to ship
to market. Beyond that, he couldn't
make any promises. In the mean time,
he went to roping contests on weekends
to entertain himself. At one of these
events, he met up with a former
employer, Colonel Zack Mulhall.
Mulhall was a wealthy rancher who

Will and actor Eddie Cantor performing at the Orpheum Theater in Winnipeg, Manitoba, in 1913.

had his own wild west show. Colonel Mulhall invited Will to come and perform at the 1904 World's Fair in St. Louis.

Thousands of people would see his roping act there. Will had no idea that one of those people would be Betty Blake. Nor did Betty Blake expect to meet up with Will. As far as she knew, he was still off traveling.

When they had dinner together after one of his performances, Will realized that he was still in love with Betty. Several months later, he sent her a letter asking her to marry him. Betty replied that she would consider his offer only if he would give up show business and settle down.

Will was tempted, but he wasn't ready to give up his life as a performer.

A familiar pose of Will Rogers in his cowboy clothes.

Too many opportunities were coming his way. For several months after the World's Fair, he had been performing daily at a theater in Chicago. Then he had the chance to go to New York City with Colonel Mulhall's Wild West Show.

When Will roped the runaway steer at the opening night of Colonel Mulhall's show in Madison Square Garden, he became a New York celebrity. He was hired to perform in theaters all over the city. Will charmed audiences with his usual rope tricks. He danced in and out of spinning lariats. He twirled his rope into huge loops thirty or forty feet wide. He even brought a horse and rider out onto the stage and roped them.

But what charmed people even more than his roping skills was Will's sense of humor. Audiences were beginning to see the side of Will that had always delighted Mary Rogers. When he began to tell jokes and stories with his slow cowboy drawl, audiences howled with laughter.

Despite his successes on stage, Will felt like something was missing from his life. More than ever, he thought about Betty Blake. One day, he traveled to Betty's home town in Arkansas and announced that he had come to marry her. He even promised to settle down.

A photo from the 1918 Ziegfield Follies. On the far left is W.C. Fields. Will is second from the left, and Eddie Cantor is second from the right.

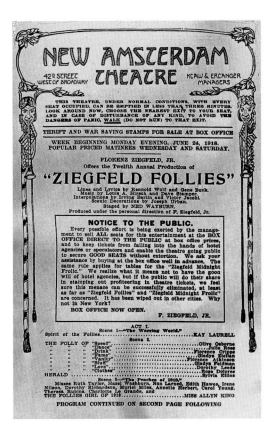

A program from the New Amsterdam Theatre where the Ziegfield Follies was presented.

This time Betty accepted. Two weeks later they were married.

Will took his new bride back to New York City where he had to finish up some show engagements. After his last performance, he was offered a bigger salary. Will was ready to turn the offer down, but Betty insisted he accept. She had been swept up in the excitement

Will and Betty Rogers were close friends of many politicans in Washington, D.C. Here they are seen on their way to visit President Calvin Coolidge.

and glamour of Will's life as a performer and no longer wanted him to quit.

But there were times when Betty did wish Will would slow down. "Years crammed full of living — that's what I like," he once told her. And that's the way he lived. A career on stage wasn't enough for Will.

In the summer of 1919, Samuel Goldwyn, a Hollywood producer, offered Will the lead role in a silent movie. At first Will was hesitant. He didn't know if he could perform without an audience in front of him. But he decided to give it a try. As it turned out, audiences loved him on the movie screen as much as they did in the theater. Goldwyn was so pleased with the first movie that he offered Will a two-year contract.

Will began his motion picture career in silent movies. He is pictured with actress Lila Lee in the photo on the left. Below is a picture from the movie A Truthful Liar.

Will decided to accept the offer and moved his family to Hollywood, California. By now, Will and Mary had four children: three sons, Will, Jr., James, and Fred, and a daughter, Mary. They needed a home. First Will bought a house in Hollywood. But after Will's youngest son Fred died from diphtheria, this home soon carried bad memories. So Will bought some land north of Hollywood and built a big

Will Rogers at home with his wife Betty and their children Jim and Mary.

A rare photo of the Rogers family together on the porch of their ranch home. Jim is 13, Bill is 17, and Mary is 15.

ranch house. For Will, the ranch was a peaceful retreat after making a movie, performing on stage, or giving a speech.

Having established himself as a performer both on the stage and in movies, Will took on new challenges that included writing a weekly column for the *New York Times*. This column was carried in newspapers throughout the United States.

(above) In 1928, Beverly Hills had no mayor. The people decided to appoint Will Rogers to be their "comedy mayor." (right) Will's radio programs were among the most popular of the time.

By 1928, Will had become so popular, that he frequently flew in government mail planes so that he could make all his engagements. A magazine editor suggested that Will was so well-liked, he could have been elected president. And maybe it was true. He got along with almost anyone. "I never met a man I didn't like," he once said.

And he never forgot those who were less fortunate. During the drought years of the 1930s, when farm families throughout the country were starving, Will organized benefit performances to help them. In eighteen days, he visited fifty cities and small towns in Texas, Arkansas, and Oklahoma, raising $225,000. In Oklahoma, he asked that part of the money be set aside for the Cherokee people.

During the early months of 1931, Will traveled around the United States to raise money for drought relief. Will is shown here at the Red Cross Headquarters with two senators before he began the tour.

Will never forgot his roots. Someday, when he was too old for show business, he hoped to return to the prairies of Oklahoma. But that day never came. On his way to Alaska in 1935, Will Rogers was killed in a plane crash.

(top, left) Will Rogers and the famous pilot Wiley Post are shown on their airplane in Fairbanks, Alaska. This was their last stop before the crash that killed them both. (bottom, left) Wiley Post's plane after the crash. (bottom, right) The front page of the Claremore Daily Progress announcing the death of Will Rogers.

In fifty-six years "crammed full of living," Will accomplished more than most people could ever dream of. Still, he was never one to brag. "If I took myself serious where would I be?" he once said. ". . . I'm still just an old cowhand at heart."

WILL ROGERS

1879 Born November 4, between Claremore and Oologah, Indian Territory
1890 Will's mother, Mary America Rogers, dies
1897 Enters Kemper Military School in Boonville, Missouri
1899 Meets Betty Blake, his future wife
1902 May — arrives in Buenos Aires to work as a cowhand
   October — sails for Durban, South Africa
   November — joins the Texas Jack Wild West Circus in South Africa
1904 Performs at St. Louis World's Fair
1905 April 27 — makes New York debut in Madison Square Garden with Colonel Mulhall
1908 November 25 — marries Betty Blake
1911 Son William Vann born
1912 Daughter Mary born
1915 Son James Blake born
1916 Joins the Ziegfeld Follies
1919 Son Fred born; Will and family head to West Coast to film his first motion picture, *Almost a Husband*
1922 December 24 — first newspaper column appears in the *New York Times*
1933 Begins nationwide radio broadcasts
1935 August 15 — killed with Wiley Post in airplane crash in Barrow, Alaska

INDEX

ABOUT THE AUTHOR

Peter Anderson studied Native American literature and history while earning an M.A. in American Studies at the University of Wyoming. He has worked as a carpenter, editor, river guide, and newspaper reporter. Currently he lives in Salt Lake City where he teaches part-time and writes. During the summer, he is a wilderness ranger with the U.S. Forest Service.